Simple Connections

OUR JOURNEY NAVIGATING AUTISM FROM THE HEART

Angie Mondragon
with
Kendra Khalil

Simple Connections: Our Journey Navigating Autism from the Heart is an imprint of Dragon Press.

Ebook ISBN: 979-8-9855003-0-1
Paperback ISBN: 979-8-9855003-1-8
Hardback ISBN: 979-8-9855003-2-5

Printed in the USA. IngramSpark

First, I would like to thank my mother Maria, who created the beautiful cover for this book, you captivated Victoria perfectly in this picture. She always enjoys observing and admiring the little things.

To my husband Miguel, for editing and translating Simple Connections, thank you for encouraging me to put together all the strategies I do with our daughter to help her be happy and independent.

To my dearest friend Kendra, my spiritual sister, you took my story and brought it to life. Thank you for helping me make Simple Connections a reality.

Finally, to my children. Thank you for reminding us we can make simple connections every day. I am so grateful to have you three in my life, guiding me and teaching me to be a better mom and person. Love you girls.

A child with autism is not ignoring you.
They are waiting for you to enter their world.

-ANONYMOUS

CONTENTS

Navigating Autism From The Heart.................................... 1

Simple Connections: The Beginning 7

A New Perspective & Attitude.. 17

Our Kids Are Our Best Teachers 23

Creating Simple Spaces 31

    Creating Simple Spaces 34

    Playroom/Sensory Room 36

    Voyagers And Sensory Time 55

    Voyagers And Home Activities 59

    Voyagers In The Kitchen.................................. 63

    Voyagers In The Bedroom 68

    Voyagers On Family Outings 70

    Voyagers At Bathroom Time 76

    Voyagers And Sleep Time Routine..................... 79

Setting The Mood 84

Recommendations And References 87

NAVIGATING AUTISM
FROM THE HEART

Our Story

This book is an account of our family's experience navigating our daughter's world. All the strategies and adaptations we have incorporated into our lives were created and continue to evolve to encourage her success. We knew early on we did not want to follow traditional ABA therapy; we tried, but it wasn't for us. Victoria needed us to see her autism in a different light. Her perceived disability was not a deficit, but rather a different ability! She needed us to believe that her individuality is a gift and her differences are incredible tools that need to be polished and guided through love and support. We realized her autistic traits, such as stimming, were a way of processing her environment; not something to be extinguished, in order to fit in. Her behaviors were a form of communication that we needed to understand, in order to assist her in learning a better way of expressing herself. Our sole purpose with Victoria's development became to help her navigate her own path, with all the support we could give and by surrounding her with love, empathy, and compassion.

My husband and I reached the conclusion that traditional school was not a choice. Having experienced how the school system works with our children, I was not a fan. There are some amazing and dedicated teachers and staff that care and work hard; but unfortunately, they are overworked and underpaid. It is the nature of bureaucracy that makes this job challenging and causes high numbers of teacher burn-out. I worked with children and young adults on the spectrum before becoming a mom and the experience led me to reflect and create our homeschool program for Victoria. My purpose was to create a stress-free environment where she could be herself and learn at her own pace.

In our quest that began four years ago, we have now come to a place where Victoria has learned to regulate her emotions, reduce meltdowns, and is now happier and more willing to participate in tasks asked of her. We believe her accelerated improvement began within weeks of discovering the recommendations of the Son-rise Program, *Autism Breakthrough* written by Raun Kaufman. This book truly has been life changing, as it altered our perspective and reaffirmed beliefs about autism. We gained a more positive outlook about Victoria's capabilities and by simply JOINING her in "her world", a term used by the Son-Rise program, she became interested in joining ours. This was the key to helping her recognize and make the common connections our family longed for.

Victoria was almost four years old and we didn't want to force her to brush her teeth, clean her hair, or eat her meals; we wanted her to understand the importance of caring for our bodies to stay healthy. She would hide in her stroller anytime we visited new places. Her lack of flexibility also extended it into the way she ate. These were just some of the connections she had difficulty making and, in addition to her sensory sensitivities, made these mundane tasks unbearable for her.

When I first discovered the Autism Breakthrough, "Joining" blew my mind! The concept had never occurred to me, yet seemed logical. This was also a time period when Victoria was non-verbal and only communicated her basic needs through simple sign language. She did not want anyone touching or playing with her or her toys. We would often find Victoria playing by herself in the corner of the living room, seemingly in a trance as she played with her figurines by lining these up or making patterns with it. If you touched her creation, she would have a meltdown; the crying and screaming would become so intense it led to gagging and vomiting. She loved wandering around the house while playing with her shadow or staring through her fingers, as she held her hand in front of her face. Sometimes Victoria would come over to us, just to see what her dad or I were doing; sometimes even run up to us briefly smiling and then running away. Changes in routine, bath time, and eating made her nervous. We could sense her distrust anytime we tried to teach her. She would run away from me, if it was time to put her shoes on. Worry over what would happen to her toys when we left our home debilitated her. Victoria seemed to enjoy outings with us, but the anxiety would creep in and win; we'd find ourselves obligated to cut the trip short in order to avoid further escalation. To see her in such distress was deeply painful. I can't really explain it, but I could feel her fear and anxiety. I could feel her sadness and all I wanted to do was take it away and make her happy. Even though our attitude towards autism and Victoria's progress had always been positive, we had many moments of struggle. Our hearts would fill up with fear when we thought of her future. Will she have the ability to communicate her needs? Will others understand her? Could we ever trust someone else with Victoria? My thoughts could go on and on about everything that scared me, pushing me to research ways to help her.

Once we started *Joining* Victoria, little by little we were blessed with small moments. Moments like the first time Victoria said "Nani", which is what she calls me. At this point, she was four and half years old and had only ever said "da-da" and "agua" for water. She came running out of her therapy room and scanning the lobby she spotted me letting out a high pitch scream, saying "NANI!". I couldn't believe it; my eyes filled up with happy tears as my ears had just heard the most amazing sound of her voice, finally calling ME! Her therapist tried to correct her, but I stopped her and explained it was the first time she had ever said "mommy". It was good enough for me and I will take it! I am Nani!

Despite my background in ABA and other strategies recommended by autism specialists, I had never thought to Join my child in her stimming. How did I do this? Well, just like you may be thinking. One afternoon, while Victoria was immersed in one of her favorites stims, spinning, I got up and spun by myself in a corner of the room near her. I was waiting and watching out of the corner of my eye for her response. The first time I did this, she did not pay any attention to me. The second time I did it, I briefly caught her attention. She stopped and looked at me; so puzzled, yet interested in my imitation of her. The third time I spun, she started to laugh and spin closer to me. When Miguel came home that evening, I told him about our interaction and in fascination he spun just a couple of times to see Victoria's smile big.

The following day, I continued to Join her in spinning, this time I sat down when I was done. What she did next brought me to tears; she came over, pulled my arms and signed "more". I asked her, ``do you want me to spin with you?" and she signed "more", clapped her hands, and jumped out of pure excitement. I spun with her and got super dizzy, but felt exhilarated over making that connection with her. I knew right away the Son-Rise program possessed the tools I could use to reach my daughter. I was already working on so much with Victoria, but hadn't been able to truly connect with her or have meaningful interactions in all our learning, until I joined her.

We started Joining everything; from how she played with her toys to how she wanted to eat her food. She thought it to be hilarious and would laugh so hard. Victoria's overall personality became so happy and positive as we were enjoying the exchanges we were having. It enabled me, in our homeschooling, to add some more challenging activities and now on her own she would participate for seconds at a time. We stayed positive and made our efforts with playful energy. This was the beginning; the key to making meaningful connections between our world and hers. Victoria started seeking us more frequently to Join her and gradually her stimming began to wane; though it hasn't gone away completely. This is certainly not what we were aiming for, as we understood it's her body's way of processing her environment; but in exchange, she opened up and started to be more present and willing to participate in everyday tasks.

Our hope is that you can take something away from our experiences. The exercises and examples in this book are in many ways an anecdote of what my husband and I did with Victoria to help her communicate and be as independent as possible at her age. Our focus is to teach her real life skills and so we believe it is crucial for her individual development to focus on simple tasks. These include dressing, eating, playing, hygiene, and her emotional health as a priority. When your child is happy everything falls into place; learning and understanding occur and connections are made throughout your home and community. When we provided Victoria a safe, relaxed space with no pressure to complete tasks, she started doing them on her own, with little to no resistance. She began to spend less time in her world and would Join us instead. It was amazing to see her change, once we changed our perspective and attitude.

We continue to be firm believers in therapy, as it is a very important part of our daughter's development. It is important to be aware that these supports will evolve as a child grows and you may add or take away services, as you see fit for your child's changing needs. However, if you are having doubts and a feeling of uneasiness over the therapies your child is doing, I recommend you listen to that feeling; don't disregard it. Bring up your concerns to your therapist and they should be able to address your questions, giving you confidence that they are helping your child make progress in the right direction. You may consider doing some more research online or listening to young adults on the spectrum, as many talk about their upbringing. These individuals will sincerely share their experience as far as what worked and what didn't work during their formative years.

I believe Victoria entered our life to make us better people, help us grow, and be able to assist other families like ours. There is no manual handed to us when the doctor gives us our child's diagnosis; we can only walk the path and learn as we go. We can use the help of other autism parents in our community, read as much as possible about sensory integration, language, play, social and emotional development, and ask the right specialists for their recommendations. Understanding it is not the therapist's sole responsibility to help our kids, WE must embrace this journey and with all the love and care we have for our voyagers. We must guide them, love them, and motivate them to be the amazing human beings they are. This is our journey; some of us are ready to take this life and roll with it, others may be scared and nervous. I believe it is essential, and part of the process, to allow yourself to feel all the anger, the sadness, the frustration and the happiness. Let yourself feel and then take action, not holding anything back and treating every day as a new opportunity.

I am grateful, for the amazing moms I have chatted with in the lobby, for the many children that have helped me understand them better, and for the wonderful therapists who think outside of the box. Because of all of them, I see a wonderful future for my daughter and hope you will too!

SIMPLE CONNECTIONS:
THE BEGINNING

It was a sunny fall day like any other in Florida, when my eyes were opened and my entire philosophy on raising my autistic daughter shifted. I got up to make breakfast! We only had one car at the time, so that meant I needed to get everyone ready because Victoria had a four-hour session at an ABA therapy center. In preparation for the day, I had to make sure she drank her protein milk and ate some breakfast before chasing her into the bathroom where I'd grab her to keep her still long enough, to then force a tooth brush into her mouth and fight her to clean her teeth. This then proceeded onto pleading with her to get dressed and put her shoes on, all while taking in her ear-piercing screams. Once our three-year-old Victoria was settled in her car seat, next to her sister Veronica who was a year old at the time, we'd drive to drop my husband off at work. On the way, our minds were already preparing for another meltdown, because Victoria had severe separation anxiety. Like clockwork, daddy would say goodbye, give her a hug and kiss, and reassure her he'd see her later that day...and BAM! The crying and screaming started again.

Needless to say, I'd be mentally and emotionally drained by the time we arrived at therapy. Victoria received Applied Behavioral Analysis Therapy, or ABA; the most common behavioral treatment for children with autism. These therapies were implemented by a Registered Behavior Technician, or RBT, who used research-based strategies to teach certain skills, as well as eliminating and replacing unwanted behaviors. Her morning had been challenging, but I had held hope the day's session would be smooth.

On days like these, I'd rarely return home while she was in session. Her baby sister and I stayed nearby, in the lobby or a few blocks from the office. Usually, Veronica and I would go to a mommy and me session, followed by Storytime at the local library, and then ending our activities at a playground near the ABA center, before circling back to pick up Victoria.

This became another one of many occasions in which I walked into the lobby greeted by her spine-chilling screams. My heart started racing. I was thinking of a million and one different things that could have triggered her. I asked one of the RBTs how long she had been upset and she politely responded, "not long, we just finished working on turn-taking and she didn't want to return the toy we gave her". I thought, "ok they've got this under control". Inching toward the area she was in, I saw her literally rolling on the ground, crying with high-pitched screams, while a circle of therapists surrounded her observing; no one was actively trying to calm her down. Not. One. Person!

I understood they had professional procedures, but here was a three-year-old little girl unable to process and articulate basic thoughts, shrieking to the top of her lungs, looking for someone to just hold her and acknowledge what she may have been feeling. I instinctively knew this is all she wanted; a hug, a sense of safety, and understanding. I stepped in, knelt next to her, and hugged her. I let her know softly in a low voice, I understood her feelings by reassuring her that I knew she was sad to let go of the toy and then reminded her it was time to go home. She couldn't communicate clearly at that time, so she would gesture or make verbal approximations, letting me know she understood. She got herself up, hugged me tightly, pointed to the door, and tried to say, "home". After this day, I knew in my gut Victoria needed a different approach. A more gentle, loving, and patient approach to help her make the simple connections we as parents want for our kids. The stoic, research-based methods we had used until then felt counterproductive to her healthy development, as a long-life learner and a voyager in her unique journey through life.

A little about myself

My name is Angie. I've traveled this path for over two decades. From the time I was a little girl, I knew I wanted to work with children and families. I remember always being intrigued by my cousin, a happy boy who had his unique way of playing and learning. He enjoyed playing with paper, as he would roll it into little balls and keep them in his pocket or store them around the house. My family, concerned that he had been diagnosed with autism, did what any parent in their shoes would do; enroll him in all kinds of services that were available, such as speech and behavior therapy. I wanted to help them, so I became my cousin's respite care therapist when he was around eight years old. This was my first experience seeing through the eyes of a child with autism; taking in details and learning about how he navigated his day with his limited communication skills at the time. He taught me a new sense of appreciation for the more simple things. This time with my cousin was the first step on my path to understanding and supporting children on the spectrum.

In my twenties, I volunteered at Schott Communities, a special organization that provides services to people with multiple disabilities. One of the many amazing divisions of Schott Communities was their St. Jude Chapel; a place of worship that was, and today continues to be, truly inclusive. While volunteering in their faith formation department, I worked with young adults on the spectrum helping them complete their religious sacraments; sacred rites in the Catholic Church that are represented by certain actions, typically taught to Catholics through a series of classes at a young age. It is a deeply religious tradition for many church families that treasure their faith. For those who had children on the spectrum, having their child receive these sacraments was particularly invaluable; as this meant they would be able to participate in daily church services, known as mass. These students were not able to attend traditional Sunday school, due to their difficulties focusing and communicating. In response, we developed a picture book, so that anyone on the spectrum could more easily concentrate and follow along during mass. We detailed every part of the mass in pictures, including entrance songs, scripture readings, communion, and prayers. We provided a visual order of actions like standing, kneeling, and when to do the sign of the cross; ultimately facilitating their participation in weekly mass. For me, it was special and significant to be part of creating these meaningful connections between students and the church community. Visuals played a key role in bridging communication and comprehension for our students and it made a life-changing impact on their lives and the lives of their families. In those years, my passion for supporting family relationships of those who have a member with autism intensified.

In pursuit of a career that would best suit my calling, I began working with children on the spectrum as a personal care assistant, a respite care therapist, a teacher assistant, a substitute teacher, and a behavior therapist, while attending college. In these various roles, I enjoyed working with families in their home, rather than at the ABA center; because changes made at home, in the family's natural environment, tended to become more permanent and thus life-changing for the child! Being home allowed everyone to be themselves without any pressure or judgment and, to me, this put parents and their kids in the best state of mind to learn and to encourage a deeper connection with their child. It was in this process; many parents became aware of their natural ability to be their children's best teacher!

When my daughter was diagnosed, my perspective on autism began to change completely! In one of the many books I read, one parent described her experience raising her child on the spectrum as constantly being on a "trial and error course" (Libutti, Awakened by Autism). I could understand, as I had tried various recommended therapies with my daughter. Being an ABA therapist by trade, I immediately began strategies in my home after her diagnosis. I worked consistently with my daughter, applying ABA methods for two full years; from the time she was 18 months until she was 3 1/2 years old. However, contrary to my experience as a therapist, I slowly began to observe how my spunky little girl had become anxious and afraid of new experiences, averse to change. I realized anxiety began affecting her deeply; her learning, her level of progress, and even her desire to be around our family in social events had noticeably decreased. It was evident to me that she was unhappy learning each day. I proceeded to dispose of all the data I had collected. I had become exhausted. Following ABA strategies at home had become unrealistic. For so many years, I had been the therapist suggesting these strategies to parents. I now found myself lacking in giving my daughter the best opportunity possible in her journey. My frustration got me thinking that there had to be a better, less forceful, more loving, and natural way of teaching her!

Simple Connections is just that! No assessments, no data collection, only making

Simple Connections throughout the day in every interaction and experience we encounter.

It is my hope you find Simple Connections helpful in simplifying everyday tasks that can seem overwhelming or impossible for our little voyagers. This approach does not mean we do away with goals, instead, we develop goals from a place of greater awareness of our child's needs and capabilities. When you are ready to jot down some goals, be mindful of the purpose, and do the goals satisfy your expectations or your child's needs? Will the goal lead towards more or less of your support? The primary goals we set for our little ones should lead to teaching safety awareness, building up their independence across your home, and ultimately lead to a happier child. Another important factor is to seek out goals that can naturally happen in your home. The more realistic and natural you can teach these goals in your home, the easier your child can learn to practice and implement them on their own at home, and in the community.

I welcome you to embark on this journey full of love and rewarding experiences. You are invested in your child and have already opened your mind to what more can be done in pursuit of guiding them to fulfilling their highest potential. Many of you have already taken the first step into this new adventure by exploring various possibilities to assist your child. As in any new journey, we must bring some basic essentials. For the suggestions in this book, you will primarily need Love and a Positive Attitude! Without these mindful attributes, whether you are new to the autism family or you are a veteran, what we are trying to achieve won't work. We as the parents, advocates, and the voice of our little voyagers are the ones who must check our attitude and remember to show love, above all things. This is especially true when our journey gets rocky and our children can perceive everything that is going on around them, though they don't let us know!

Becoming aware of our intentions

I briefly served as a consultant in an elementary school, where I was to provide support to ESE Teachers working with children on the spectrum. During my visit, I noticed different objects in bins meant for a 10- year-old student. The activity set before him was to screw washers onto a large screw that was bolted to a wooden plank. I asked the teacher what the child was learning. She stated it was an activity to build independence. I asked myself how this was helping to build independence.

In my opinion, it didn't! He was learning how to complete a specific task on his own, screwing on washers, while it was strengthening his fine motor muscles. However, it seemed to me it would be challenging for a child to use this skill in transitioning toward independence unless he would be working at a job that required him to do that specific task in the future. A myriad of activities could have served him better to complete tasks independently, while strengthening their fine motor muscles such as matching and folding socks or wiping and stacking chairs after lunch.

Take a moment to reflect on this previous example and think about this student's future. All our kids should be familiar with putting their dirty clothes in a hamper and putting it away after it's washed. If not, guess what? It's time to take the opportunity to teach this simple task; we are teaching our children independence through tasks they will need to be doing as adults. This can be taught in stages and supported by activities, such as matching socks, folding shorts, or sorting clothes. This is the mindset I want you to be in when you look at your child's goal; will that activity chosen to meet the goal benefit their independence into the future?

So, what might this look like in practice at home? In our house, for example, Victoria and her younger sisters help sort the whites, lights, and dark-colored clothes into the laundry baskets. They then take turns helping me carry the basket to the laundry room, where there is a step stool for them to reach over the washer and throw in the clothes. This is excellent heavy work and great sensory input at their young age. I then measure the detergent into a cup and one of them helps me pour it in, close the lid, and press start. Sometimes they may fight over who gets to push the button, which then becomes an opportunity to talk about turn-taking and giving others a chance to lead. When it's time to move clothes to the dryer, I take the wet heavy clothes out of the washer and hand them to one of the girls to put them into the dryer. My youngest daughter then closes the door and the middle princess pushes the start button. When it is time to fold, they participate to the best of their ability and then put their clothes away with a little help. Phew!

This whole thing may not be perfect but we are not looking for perfection; we want them to enjoy the activity and do their best to complete it. I must admit, Victoria does not like this. She likes folding, but not putting her clothes away. So, we make it a game; whoever is the fastest to put their item away first, wins a chocolate chip cookie! Throwing in rewards to engage and encourage your child if they need it, is important. We do the laundry routine weekly because I consider it to be a really important life skill. My girls are six, four, and two years old, so for me, this is one of the activities I have found we can do together. This was just my example. There may be other responsibilities you can think of to involve your child every week. Maybe it can be teaching them to take out the trash, clean up a room, make a simple meal, and so on. Once you have an idea in mind, break it down into steps, making it easy for you to help your child in your own way as needed. Make it a mission to let your kids join in activities that you know will benefit them in the long term and teach them to be responsible in the process. Let's use such opportunities to set goals that encourage our child to work on activities that lead to more challenging skill development, like cooking, self-care, organizing, and even conversational skills and more. We are not alone; you and I together can continually explore possibilities in our proximity and within our home life that can be used to teach our children in more meaningful ways. You Got This!

EXERCISE

The checklist on the next page is to help you brainstorm some goals you'd like your child to achieve.

Remember, the purpose of the exercise is to become aware of our intentions.

Here are some of the questions to keep in mind as you go through the exercise:

1. Is this goal for my child's developmental benefit? Or, is it a norm or milestone recommended at their age?

2. Is the goal to work towards my child's overall independence?

3. Is the goal for selfish motives?

Just think! When our kids learn skills that make them happy, it naturally builds their self-esteem and encourages them intrinsically to keep learning and applying acquired abilities to their everyday life. It's not about us; we need to take our feelings, our pride, and our desires out of the equation. Focus on what our children's needs are now for their future. Our role is to encourage their independence and allow them to explore their interests.

WHAT GOALS DO YOU WANT TO WORK ON WITH YOUR VOYAGER?

Goal	Who will benefit from the goal?	
	Child	You

 Every day is an opportunity

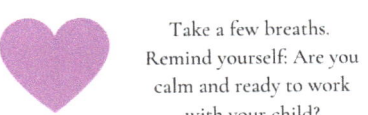 Take a few breaths. Remind yourself: Are you calm and ready to work with your child?

 Seize that opportunity whenever possible and have fun.

CAPTAIN'S REVIEW

Now that you've jotted down some goals, take a second glance at them and remember; goals should be led by your child, not just by a therapist or the ideal standards imposed by others in regards to development. Those standards should be used as references to guide you, rather than pressure you. Every single one of our voyagers is on their own path and this implies they are also on their own time.

In our family, taking one moment at a time each day is sometimes more valuable than making Victoria finish an activity she doesn't prefer. She has never really learned by using excessive prompting, as a strategy to complete something. If anything, this has harmed her by causing anxiety levels to skyrocket; which we have addressed with sensory activities. In the next chapters, we will further discuss why sensory activities are a part of our daily routine and play a key role in creating the positive environment we want our voyagers to thrive in. In fact, almost anyone can experience benefits from sensory breaks, and like all my daughters, demonstrate improvement in their mood almost immediately! It leads to a positive tone in our home and keeps me in my best state of mind to support Victoria and her sisters.

A NEW PERSPECTIVE
& ATTITUDE

A little bit about my family

In the spring of 2014, we were overjoyed expecting our first little one, Victoria. Many of us, as first-time parents, do lots of reading on what birth plan to have; whether we prefer a doctor or midwife, hospital or home birth, and so on. Certainly, whichever plan we feel is right for us, usually turns out to be the best plan. I had done my research and was adamant that I wanted a home birth; so, we found a midwife and attended the required birthing classes. They were great! In my opinion, the best class any parent could ever take.

During our prenatal classes, the midwife held out an 18-inch piece of yarn and began to tell us that the yarn represents 18 years of your child's life. She explained, "the first 4 inches of this string being the first four years are the most crucial years of your baby's life. These are the years when you influence your child the most, as by age 5, they begin their educational journey in school; where they will be influenced by teachers, school staff, peers, and possibly strangers. Your influence will no longer be the most significant, since both parents typically work and the hours left in the day before bedtime are few". Then she asked, "how would you do differently, to be the most loving and influential parents you could possibly be, with the time you have with your baby?". Miguel and I had learned what I consider to be one of the most important lessons in our lives.

Why am I sharing this? It is the moment that our journey began with Victoria, it was the first change in our perspective and attitude towards what we wanted our family to be. It wasn't easy, but we decided to live with one income, so I could stay home for the first couple of years prior to putting Victoria in school. Crazy, I know, especially with how expensive the cost of living is now. We had to do some extreme budgeting, but we did it!

It has been six years and I continue to feel gratitude for being able to stay home for my girls. Back then, it was the first time we thoughtfully changed our mindset as to how we thought life was "supposed" to be. I had originally planned to continue working and place my child in school, as it was the way I grew up. I cannot explain the intuitive feeling I had in my heart while I was pregnant, but the midwife's question, "how would you do differently to be the most loving and influential parents you could possibly be with the time you have with your baby?" just confirmed what I knew in my heart and had not yet been able to express.

Now I can affirm that changing this one perspective, changed the quality of time we spent as a family. It also transformed our attitude towards how we wanted to teach our children. We decided, shortly after Victoria was born, that we would try out homeschooling her. We didn't know then how important individualizing her education was going to be for her emotional and educational development. Now, seeing our kids bloom, especially Victoria, learning and exploring on their own validates our changing the norm. You may not be able to stay home full time with your child; however, do not underestimate the great impact you have on them despite the number of minutes you are able to dedicate. It is important that you realize every minute counts.

Our perspective and attitude can be adjusted on a large scale, as it happened to me at first; but make no mistake, it has been the small-scale changes in perspective and attitude that have made an impact on our children's lives. It is the opportunities we seize on the daily, the moments we consciously engage in, and the intention we place behind each interaction with our girls that create this impact. It is in these instances that we can choose our own perspective and attitude. This is why I consider one of the main tools you will need on this journey to have a positive and flexible attitude, conducive to becoming more intentional in creating meaningful teaching moments. It will make a difference! Believe me, doing the laundry myself would have been a lot faster; but, after some thought and change in perspective, I knew letting my girls help was going to benefit them long term. As I described in the laundry activity, age does not keep a child from learning; we can adapt any steps to our child's abilities in order to encourage them to complete any activity.

Remember, we do not need an activity to be done perfectly; instead of perfection, we want participation! It took my placing personal feelings aside and making a conscious choice to change my attitude, in order to teach my girls an important life skill. Yes, my change in attitude included a large dose of patience and creativity to get my girls involved! You may think you don't have the patience and creativity; but please, trust me when I tell you that you will find these attributes within you once you set your mind on an important skill you feel your child needs to learn. Mindset and focus have a way of strengthening us when it is fueled by the love and motivation to improve our child's quality of life. One moment at a time, it then becomes easier to alter our perspective and attitude. Think of attitude as putting on new sunglasses with a bluish tint, that will definitely make us see the world very differently. We will need this analogy to remind us to check our attitude when working with our voyagers on this journey, because how we feel and how we interact with them throughout their experiences factors into their success!

The diagram on the next page is intended to help you recall factors that will affect our journey with our child. I liken our role as parents to being captains of a ship, helping our voyagers navigate the world around them.

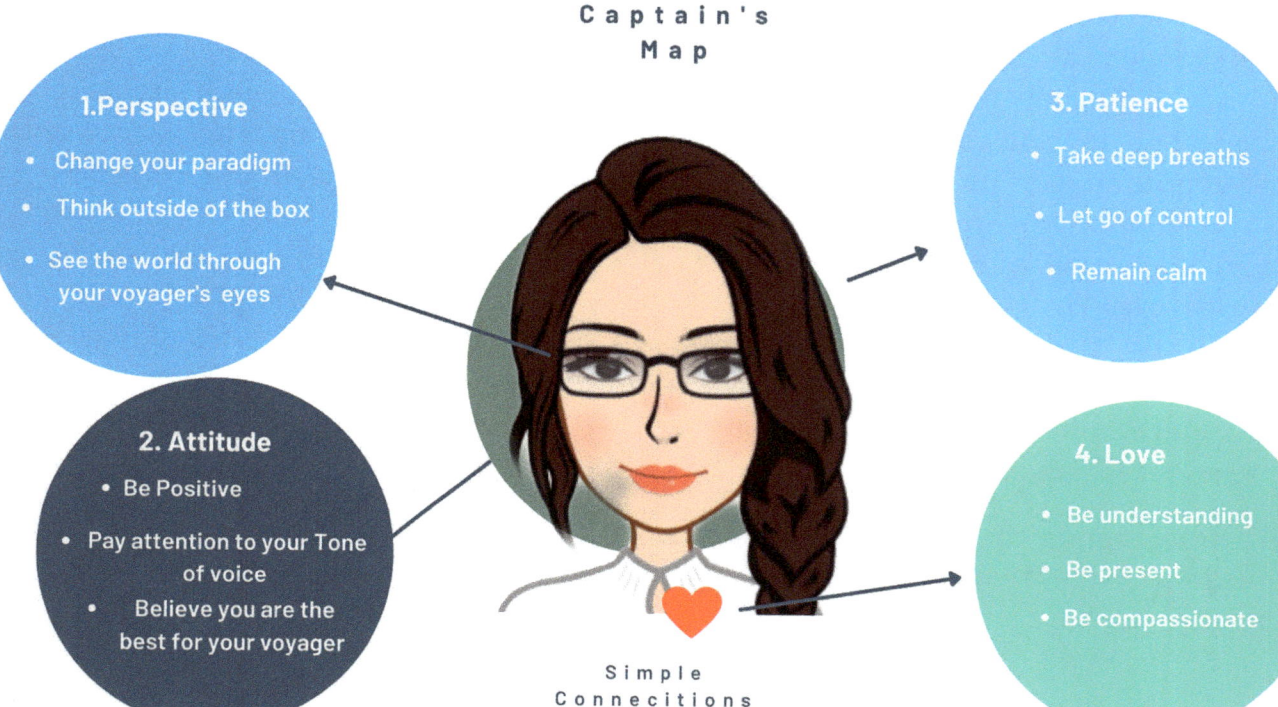

Captain's Map

1.Perspective

- Change your paradigm
- Think outside of the box
- See the world through your voyager's eyes

2. Attitude

- Be Positive
- Pay attention to your Tone of voice
- Believe you are the best for your voyager

3. Patience

- Take deep breaths
- Let go of control
- Remain calm

4. Love

- Be understanding
- Be present
- Be compassionate

Simple Connecitions

CAPTAIN'S CHECKLIST

Perspective can have an effect on our feelings.
(Are my feelings sincere or am I pretending to be happy to get by? How can I improve my perspectives?)

Attitude is the most important factor in maintaining a positive relationship with our voyager.
(How can I improve my attitude?)

Creating meaningful experiences is crucial in building permanent skills.
(How can I improve on the creation of meaningful experiences in life skills, no matter how menial or vital these may be?)

OUR KIDS ARE OUR BEST TEACHERS

I may be far from being an expert, but thankfully my daughter has been and continues to be my best teacher. When I introduce something to her, I have learned to follow her lead by first gaging her interest and her desire to want to participate. If she shows me interest, I can proceed; but if she is showing me resistance, I know to pause. Victoria has taught me to slow down and use my intuition to better connect with her. This is what I believe encourages her to open up and then allows me opportunities to join in and teach her at her level.

Our ability to actively listen, by observing and responding accordingly, to what our child is communicating to us with words or actions, and realizing that we are on their time, is key to better supporting their individual needs. These two skills are intertwined in many ways, as truly listening may take longer than we expect. We may find ourselves investing additional time in giving our child the freedom to learn to communicate and process their feelings, as they feel comfortable in various circumstances. Here's what I have learned so far.

Expanding our listening skills

Most of our voyagers have difficulty expressing themselves. Some may use words and others may express their feelings through other means like screaming or laughing, crying or giggling, jumping up out of excitement, and in other unique ways. As an example, some may also hit, while others might hug and squeeze. The important lesson for us to remember is that any behavior is a form of communication that we must actively listen to.

Victoria would cover her eyes, cry, and make loud whining noises over again when things didn't go her way. She would also rub her fingers; a physical sign of anxiety that let me know she was stressed. It often occurred when she had to put her favorite toys away before heading to speech therapy. I knew it was not therapy she had a hard time with because she enjoyed the sessions. So, this helped me deduce it was leaving the toys that likely caused her distress. I would acknowledge her feelings and assure her the toys would be in the same place when we returned home; but giving her this assurance did little to calm her down back then.

At the time, Victoria was about four years old and non-verbal; we discovered she was drawn to music and so it started playing a key role in much of our interaction. I quickly learned to attract her attention, and many times calmed her down, by turning many of the things I needed to tell her into a song. I would think of familiar tunes, such as "The Farmer in the Dell", and would change the words into the direction I was trying to give her. I'd sing, "it's time to clean up, it's time to clean up, oh yes, oh yes, oh yes, it's time to clean up!". This would make her relax a bit and she'd slowly start helping me put her toys away; it naturally helped develop her language, as she attempted to sing along. I would expand the tune to "where does this go...oh yes, oh yes, oh yes, In the bin!". Soon after doing it a few times, she began repeating the last word, "bin ", back to me, while we put the toys in the bin. Afterwards, we'd make our way to the car to drive to therapy and by then I had changed the words of the tune once again to fit the actions, "It's time to go to Speech...". I made everything I could into a song and it was a hoot! It would help her become calm and it made our transitions from cleaning up and getting to therapy much more enjoyable. Although I must admit it was exhausting for me, it was certainly all worth the effort to create these positive experiences.

When Victoria wanted to request, and she began using more words, we alternated between some basic sign language, pointing, and visuals for basic communication. As she became comfortable requesting familiar items, we then taught her to point to simple pictures of faces with feelings and simple words to describe her feelings; sad, mad, or happy to then expand that to "I am (feeling)", using a picture board. This picture board hung in our home near the kitchen, where she frequently played; and we made sure to use it almost daily, until it became her habit to grab the board every time, she needed to express her feelings.

Today, she is almost seven years old and she can communicate in full sentences with some reminders. I can attest to the fact that it all began with listening, by thoughtfully observing her behavioral cues, and learning to respond in ways that she could acknowledge. When she gets frustrated, she still needs a quick reminder to calm down and to use her words, instead of crying or whining. This gives her relief by assuring her she can return to her activities later in the day. Our journey continues to be a work in progress, but as we continue to actively listen, we feel we continue to become better equipped to support her needs.

Some children may flip out when it's time to get dressed. The screams and flailing may throw off any parent thinking, "here we go again...", but in fact this is an opportunity to step back and observe what is really triggering the child. Is it the texture of the clothes, the wrong outfit that's causing stress, or is it because it's a way to resist when it's time to go somewhere? As a parent, it is key to identify this trigger in order to help our child the right way. We do this by actively listening, observing and responding accordingly.

Let's use this example and break down how to help our child turn this circumstance into a positive experience. Let's say that through observation, we have figured out it's the texture of the clothing that is uncomfortable. If the child is sensitive to textures or the fit isn't right, the solution would be to only make available the clothes that are comfortable to them. If we observe it to be a control issue and the child refuses to wear it because it's not what they want or picked out for themselves, you can offer two choices and grant them control over their selection. It may be something very unique to the child that is making them overreact. But how else would we know, except for intently observing their behavior and the possible triggers. Only then, can we effectively attempt solutions to ease their frustrations.

Victoria has definitely battled me when it's time to get dressed, or undressed, and changed into pajamas in the evenings. She went through a phase in which she would only wear dresses. Nowadays she will not even touch a dress and that's fine with me. I have no problem letting her choose her own outfits as wild as they may look as long as they are appropriate for the weather. Also, she has never worn new clothing; if it didn't come out of her closet or her drawers, she will not wear the item. What did I do about this? I first wash the new clothing, then I sneak it into her wardrobe, as if it had always been there. When she sees it in her closet, though it may be unfamiliar, she is more accepting of the new clothing and may wear it immediately. If she doesn't wear the new items right away, I give her time and provide her with outfit choices that include new and old options. This helps her gradually transition into her new sizes as well *(her sisters, on the other hand, jump with excitement at the sight of new outfits)*.

What behaviors does your child have and what do you suppose they may be trying to communicate? In what ways do you think you could respond to help them ease frustrations and possibly expand their ability to self-regulate emotions, deal with changes, and expand their communication skills. You know your child best, so trust your instincts. When your child is crying or acting out of their norm, remember they are not being difficult, but communicating through their behavior. Remember that our children often don't know how to appropriately make requests. Show them how by repetition and modeling words and actions which will make a difference in the long run. Your child, like mine, may be verbal until anxiety and panic attacks kick in and the ability to process and verbally communicate go out the window. Even if your child is able to speak, they can benefit from learning a variety of different ways to regulate their feelings such as taking deep breaths or counting down. Be Present! Many times, we may forget to stop and take time to be mindful, rather than rushing through our day. It is arguably the most valuable gift you can give to your child. Dishes need to get done, food needs to be made, and little mouths may need help eating, in addition to work and life. Many times, all they need is a brief moment acknowledging your voyager's frustration and responding with empathy as best we can.

You are on the Child's Time, not yours

We need to make the effort to be on their time as we expand our ability to better listen and communicate with our child. To be honest, this was the challenge for me. I had to change my own expectations when working with Victoria. I found myself slowing down and letting go of any pressure to get her to do things. Our kids do not have a sense of time. Besides being hungry and aware of mealtimes, they are not necessarily aware that we follow a clock. Our kids may not know our schedule to get things done; when we eat, play, sleep, go to the bathroom, and work. Most kids wake up and want to play! If this is the case for you, seize that opportunity whenever possible and have fun! You may have to squeeze in these special moments on weekends and after school, but consider it is worth all your effort and conscious intention. Play is one of the easiest times to engage in meaningful teaching moments and many experts agree that children learn valuable lessons naturally while they're playing!

We may need to address at other times certain challenges that are unique to our child; those specific challenges that arise when we're out in public and can feel overwhelming. If you can think of such an instance, know that this is an opportunity to help your child overcome these challenges at home first! For example, Victoria had challenges getting her hands or clothing dirty. If juice or food-stained her shirt or her hands, she would stop whatever she was doing, start screaming so that the entire neighborhood could hear, and try to rip off her clothes. You can only imagine how it went for us at birthday parties and restaurants. One of the ways we worked on her overcoming this obstacle was introducing her to different messy activities at home that helped her build tolerance to getting her hands dirty. We encouraged her to play with paint and shaving cream, while providing her a towel in sight and teaching her to use it. This gave her assurance that if she was becoming overwhelmed, she could easily wipe herself. Such a small accommodation, practical for her to use anywhere she goes, helped her build knowledge and trust that there was a simple solution to ease her severe exasperation with getting messy.

We gradually improved our efforts by intentionally observing her behaviors to understand what she tried to communicate. Other times, when Victoria showed signs of feeling upset while doing a challenging activity, we'd let her know it was okay to stop; yes, Stop! This did not mean we wouldn't try again, or that I gave up and put everything away. It meant that I would pause to acknowledge her feelings and state of mind. Together we would go through deep breathing and counting exercises and pick a sensory tool to help her relax; going to her body sock, trampoline, or rocker. This quick break gave her a few moments to process her feelings and calm down. It typically took 5 to 10 minutes of break time before we could continue. Pausing this way was worth it because once she was relaxed, her calm state of mind made it easy to transition back into the messy activity. Being on her time, her pace, was vital in the process. In the following chapters, you'll find suggestions for sensory breaks that may suit your child, including large tools as well as smaller handheld portable gadgets that your child can carry with them.

When Victoria was taking a break from an activity, it was also a moment for me to compose myself; to take a quick and much-needed mommy break, if I needed to. A few deep breaths and a sip of tea did the job for me on most days. However, sometimes I wasn't able to go back to the activity with Victoria because she had lost interest after the break or because of typical daily interruptions: and that's okay!

LIST AND REFLECT ON YOUR OBSERVATIONS OF YOUR CHILD'S BEHAVIOR:

What behavior do you see?	What do you believe your child is trying to communicate?

 Every day is an opportunity

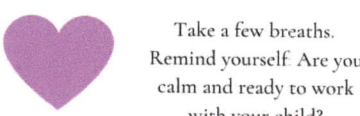 Take a few breaths. Remind yourself: Are you calm and ready to work with your child?

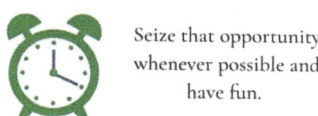 Seize that opportunity whenever possible and have fun.

CAPTAIN'S CHECKLIST

☐ Am I actively listening by observing and responding accordingly?

☐ Am I allowing my child time to process and communicate their way?

☐ Am I discovering new ways to address my child's needs, based on my observations?

CREATING SIMPLE SPACES

Our Home! Our home is filled with many things: toys, food, snacks, furniture, TVs, everyone's personal things, lots of noise and laughter and more toys. Autism has its beautiful side such as, the joy and appreciation for the simple things. At the same time the simple things can cause frustration, especially when everyday tasks are more complicated and difficult for our voyager. In turn, it can disrupt our home and our family relationships.

Your Home should be a happy, safe, and thriving environment. We have to switch how we think about everything. Honestly, it's that easy. Remember, every day is a learning opportunity! It's ok if our little one is having an off day, week, or month. We have expectations on how things are supposed to be and when they are supposed to happen. But why? Our kids are on their own schedule, their own journey that we get to be a part of. We should also be that flexible and open to the same change. When we change the attitudes we may have towards certain behaviors, that is when we see how brilliantly everything unfolds and our kids can flourish.

Creating Your Space

We embraced her individuality and encouraged her to freely be herself at home. Victoria then began to join us and to shed some of that anxiety that had built up in her. It may sound like a no-brainer. For us, it meant we gradually transformed the environment of our home to incorporate sensory-friendly spaces to better suit her needs, clear boundaries that helped her understand rules and safety, and the thoughtful layout of furniture and toys to help her make better use of the space and enable her independence. Although not an immediate change, the small adjustments made with Victoria in mind assisted us with her learning needs, her personality, her emotional well-being and her health.

As we began to understand our daughter in a deeper way, we realized she needed to jump frequently, sought pressure, squeeze items throughout the day, and at times wanted quiet hiding places. Among many other idiosyncrasies, she also required extra help to learn important life skills. It became evident we could not meet her needs in traditional ways. We met her needs by having her watch us do our daily routines or by giving her directions, as most parents do at home. However, as we began to alter certain spaces by moving furniture, adding simple accommodations, and communicating concepts in more tangible ways, she began to flourish in so many areas! By letting her be herself, while meeting her at her level, she expanded her language, she was motivated to try new things and was more flexible. Unique arrangements can also be made in your home to encourage your child to be themselves and thrive! It will take time. However, ideas will come to you that will benefit their development in countless ways if you begin to focus on the goals that you've set for your child and take the time to interact with them in an effort toward those goals. In this section, I'm sharing with you what has worked with our daughter, Victoria, in regards to the things we changed in our home to accommodate and encourage her growth. It's not set in stone, as we sometimes change things around depending on her preferences or on what we're wanting to teach her. The idea is to show you examples and inspire you to make changes in your home environment that may help your child.

As a quick sidenote, it is important that you have resources available to you, should you need to make additional investments toward your child's development. Victoria, for example, is the recipient of a scholarship that allows me to purchase items, equipment, and services. Every state has its own support system for families that have children with special needs. In the State of Florida, it's The Family Empowerment Scholarship. You can find more information by visiting, www.stepupforstudents.org. For most states, you can also do a general search online for such services or visit your local school board website to get in touch with the right department.

CREATING SIMPLE SPACES

Quiet Space

We created a quiet space for Victoria to go to when she needed to calm down, when she seemed anxious, or when she just needed a quiet moment. It became the space where we practiced deep breathing. I showed her face-to-face, step by step how to take deep breaths and imitate my actions. She would only watch me in the beginning, but within months, she began to copy what I intentionally showed her. The key was to be consistent in taking her to the space until she understood it was simply a safe spot for her to decompress or enjoy some quiet.

At the moment Victoria continues to go to this space at home. However, we have now gone a step beyond and begun teaching her that when no "quiet space" is available, she can still give herself a break by closing her eyes and practicing her deep breaths. Showing her that this method can be used anywhere was crucial. However, Victoria

clearly needed to first learn the skill in a quiet and comfortably familiar place, before she could learn to calm herself anywhere else or in any other situation outside of our home.

It all began with showing her a physical space that eventually made sense as a place to emotionally recover and also gave her time to understand how to calm down. The added benefit of continuing to gain this important life skill, giving herself quiet breaks to refocus and relax, is that Victoria is also gaining greater self-awareness of her own needs.

Quiet Space

If you need to plan a quiet "cooling down" spot for your child, feel free to follow these tips along with any unique adjustments your child may benefit from.

- Create or designate a specific area, easily accessible in your home that is quiet and free of distractions.

- Sensory bins and items are a great tool; you can have a basket labeled "Calming Down" and maybe a picture that represents that for your child. Fill the bin with sensory gadgets and tools.

  - Sensory gadgets can include: squishy toys, body brushes, spinners, stretchy bands, etc.

  - Sensory tools can include a weighted blanket, ear muffs, sunglasses, etc. (Customize how you see fit. You know your little one best)

- Be a model and show your child what to do. Get eye level with them and show them breathing, counting down, or the strategy you prefer; then have them copy what you do until they are able to do it on their own.

  - Keep it simple. Don't talk about what got your child upset until they calm and are ready to communicate.

  - The idea is to make this skill transferable to any circumstance, so that your child is able to self-regulate anywhere.

- Visuals help increase comprehension and communication. These can be in the form of short social stories, boards, or individual cards.

  - A short story about calming down (speech therapists can assist with these)

  - A board showing the steps to calming down.

  - Individual pictures showing the steps to calming down.

PLAYROOM/SENSORY ROOM

Here are some tips that may help you set up a space at home. These suggestions are meant to guide you and can be adapted with any unique adjustments your child may need.

As you can see in the picture, it was important for us that our space be multi-purpose. It is divided into three main sections, a reading nook, a play and sensory corner, and a spot for art.

Reading Nook

- Keep your books in a basket on the floor or on a low shelf, for easy access.

- Have board books easily accessible for younger voyagers so that they are not drawn to books you want to preserve.

- Rotate your books, themes are so much fun and keep your little one interested in reading.

- This is the place where we also practice how to care for library books by keeping a designated bin.

Play and Sensory Space

- Try cubed shelving; it is ideal for bins, easy organization, and fast location of items.

- Keep your set up simple with three to four bins, or sections on your shelf to encourage sorting and cleaning up toys independently.

- Have toys and activities that interest your child

- Remember to be thoughtful about pretend play and do not feel obligated to have such items if it is not meaningful for your child.

- Provide a basket or bin for those favorite items that do not fit in a toy category, so that your child learns where to access and store independently.

- Have a plan to practice some simple turn taking with your child daily.

Art Spot

- A standing or table easel may help your child to more easily focus on their creations.

- Have a sensory bin you can fill it with kinetic sand and other sensorial materials (more examples in sensory chapter, page 55).

- Rocking chair can be for reading, writing, relaxing, as well as vestibular input, which supports balance.

Other Items:

- Gel Tiles are great for pretending to play with lava or water and visual stimulation.

  - Kids love to squish, jump and walk on it!

  - Consider a hammock chair swing, which helps with balance and body awareness.

  - TV may be important for music, movies, and other educational purposes.

Play and Sensory Spaces

Play rooms and/or Sensory spaces are essential for healthy development, as it is well known that children learn through play. This area should create many opportunities to practice developmental skills and provide the sensory input they may need through PLAY. This includes a variety of activities like building with blocks or other items, pushing cars or play strollers, pulling toys, and many other toys that engage your child and allow for you to join in taking turns. Notice how sensory is more than lights and music; it is also by building, pushing, and pulling that your child is getting sensorial input. It is up to you and your creativity, based on your child's particular needs.

Some families may prefer to have less items in a space so as to not overwhelm the child; maybe there are too many toys, making choices difficult for them. Maybe too many items are causing emotional outbursts; such as being overly excited to the point they can't focus on one activity for more than a minute or being so under stimulated they don't want to play with anything. Here is where the motto, *"less is more"*, will come into play. Other families may be able to create an environment with a greater variety of toys and activities. Either way, the important thing for you to remember is that your child learns through play! It will provide many great benefits, including academic practice, emotional and social development, increased focus, sensorial and physical input, gross and fine motor improvement, and of course, fun!

Having bins labeled with pictures or words helps organize you and your child. Simple category labels, like blocks, cars, animals, and figurines make it easy to find and put away toys. This "categorizing" task alone helps reinforce executive functioning, strengthens focus, and is even a precursor to reading. Most importantly, it is teaching our little one a useful life skill. If you were to use this method of organizing toys you may find, as I have, that rotating toys is crucial in helping minimize boredom or obsessions with certain toys. It also helps to keep rigidity at bay. Sometimes Victoria will start obsessing over a toy, specifically dinosaurs or small animal figurines. To avoid her anxiety or obsession with the item, I will remove it from the playroom for a couple of weeks then re-introduce it at another time. "Rigidity" is a characteristic we all share in common to some degree and for many children with ASD, it is a way of exercising control over the familiarity they desire. There isn't anything particularly wrong with it, unless it affects their flexibility and adaptation to new situations. Our goal is to help our children have positive experiences and teach them how to create adjustments when they need it, by first assisting them with these small challenges at home. For example, I like to rotate toys depending on the activities we have planned or skills we want to work on. If I wanted Victoria to work on sharing, (with her sisters or cousins), I would place a pretend tea set in her toy rotation that week in place of her dinosaurs. Thus, I eliminate her tendency to obsess on her favorite toys and provide her with the opportunity to explore and learn sharing. No, it's not as easy as it sounds, as I often assist when it's her turn to share or wait. You can think out of the box to help your child overcome their challenges too and with your help, they will thrive.

Finally, consider having toys in your play space that serve a specific purpose for your child. Do not eliminate those unique items some of our voyages may like playing with; for example, straws, string, paper for shredding (one of Victoria's favorite activities), and other items that may not be considered toys. Remember, such items are fascinating and may be of great interest to some children; they may be exploring or it may simply bring them comfort. Nevertheless, it is an opportunity for us to embrace their individuality and to put on our blue shades to see it their way!

Perspective on Pretend Play

Pretend play is another fun way to engage our children. Though it may sound a bit intimidating for some parents, it is actually a very natural form of play! Children will typically play imitating many of the things they see their parents or people on TV do. Thus, most pretend toys are versions of real-life tools and costumes. Many believe "pretend" playing is important to develop imagination and creativity. However, it certainly is not a one size fits all activity and many children may not prefer it. If your little one doesn't quite play this way, but you'd like to expose them to it, you can take one of their favorite toys and show them how to pretend with it. Let's say your child enjoys any type of blocks. Sit with them to build a simple tower and teach them to pretend a big wind blew it down, for example. If that is too basic, then try building things that lend to easy pretending like building a car, a space-ship, or even a city to encourage their imagination. Show them how to play and then praise them when they make their attempts. Another example, would be pretending to make a meal with play items; you can make a soup and cook it in a pot, pretend to cut fruit, or build a sandwich and have a picnic.

Try to meet your child at their level as best you can. If this type of pretending is not appropriate for them, then choose activities that can be extended beyond pretend play to real life skills. Let them play with real tools: for example, banging pots on the floor while you make dinner. Maybe your voyager is a more practical and visual learner who would rather make a real sandwich or have some juice and cookies in a real tea party with you. Maybe you are washing dishes and they are around you; provide a sponge and kitchen towel and show them how to clean their own plate and utensils until they can do it on their own each evening. Some children may enjoy sorting clean utensils back in a drawer rather than pretending to cut pretend food. If you follow me here, the point is that if pretend play is not meaningful for your child, especially in the preschool years (when all the experts are suggesting it's important), it's okay to allow them to use some real tools, so long as it is safe. It's okay to do some real-life activities they can better relate to and provide them with useful life skills in the process.

Perspective on Sharing Toys

We must consider our child's abilities, when thinking of creating opportunities for our voyager to share and play by taking turns with others. If this is difficult for them, we must remember to let our child pick what they want to play with in order to start on a positive note and increase their chances of success with sharing. Do not force them in any way to play with a child or adult they don't seem comfortable with, as it can send the wrong message to your child. As parents, we can perceive who our child is drawn to, as well as who they resist, and it is important to honor and validate their feelings and preferences. Also, do not make your voyager share their most precious toy or object; all this will do is upset them and forfeit any meaningful experiences. Start with  neutral items such as things that are easy for them to separate from.

When I was helping my daughter to learn to share, I would have a bin with different sized and textured balls; a toy that was neutral for Victoria and that made it easy to play reciprocally by throwing or rolling the ball to each other. Now, matchbox cars happen to be a hit with my girls; when we play, I create a simple race track using painter's tape to section off the start and finish lines, and also tape off a "waiting area" for the cars. This gives Victoria a clear visual cue of where the cars are supposed to start, finish, and where to "wait" for turns on the track. Sometimes, one turn on the track is all she can take and to me, it's awesome; but other times, if she and her sisters are super excited and into it, they have played making the cars take turns for hours. I believe the repetition of making the cars take turns on the track has helped Victoria immensely in learning to wait and take turns in other opportunities outside of play. The key is to find the toy or activity that will specifically work for your voyager and practice it frequently.

Reading Nook

Having a reading nook in your space will automatically draw your child to books and encourage reading, so long as you have books, they're interested in. It will increase your opportunities to curl up with your child and enjoy stories. It is the place for our daily quality time and the easiest way for me to provide my daughters with essential skills. According to Marie Rippel from All About Reading Press, the reading program I use with Victoria, reading aloud to children at any age can create a special one-on-one bond, aid in increasing attention span, assist in developing language and imagination, and building comprehension. I love that I don't have to think about how to teach these skills!

If you have difficulty getting your child to sit with you to enjoy a book, begin with little steps. Start by finding the book they are most drawn to and sit them on your lap. If they cannot sit through the entire story, read only their favorite parts each day. The key is to do it daily because your child will slowly begin to sit for longer periods. They will gradually increase their focus when you read to them, and eventually you will be able to introduce new and longer books. Don't give up! Just remember that reading aloud is one of the best skill building activities you will ever do for your voyager.

Art Spot

Art time is hands down one of the most favorite activities in our home. Not only is it wonderful for sensory input and perception, but art is essential for our child's self-expression. In our home, we have an easel for painting to give the girls free reign over their creations. They have choices to use watercolors, tempera paint, crayons, or markers. Some children on the spectrum may not know what to do, other than scribble or mix paint colors until it's a murky mess. It's okay, Victoria started out just like this. She would dip the paint brush into all the paints and just brush in one spot until the paper ripped. I would just remove the ripped paper and give her a new sheet. Eventually, Victoria started drawing and painting shapes to make pictures. This has further progressed to some very unique creations.

I feel it's important to mention that some parents may not like messes, let alone having paint used in their home. I want to remind you; we are changing our perspective and attitudes towards our beliefs on helping our child get through life on the spectrum. Just as we are helping them with adjustments, so must we with our own behaviors and actions. We must get over our discomforts and move forward in order

to create this kind of positive welcoming environment for our children; one in which they can be free to explore using all their senses. If the possibility of a mess is something you need to adjust to, maybe doing art in the kitchen, patio, or garage can make cleaning up easier. Limiting the number of materials, you have out at one time can also help. Another alternative is to download painting Apps for children to your home tablet. This is something we also do on occasion and have found it is very beneficial. We have a stylus pen so that Victoria can practice her grasp while drawing and coloring.

Some supplies you may want to keep stocked at home are washable paints, paint brushes, paper for painting and paper for coloring, crayons, markers, stickers, safety scissors, and glue-sticks. If you feel making this sort of free art is not benefiting your child and you want to show them a more structured way of making meaningful art, there are some simple approaches you can take. For example, making art inspired by your child's favorite books to read. It is an easy and fun way to bring art and reading together. You can pick a character or favorite animal from the story, you can trace it, print it out, or let them draw it. If your child is a beginner, they are most likely working on creating lines and diagonals or simple shapes like triangles, squares, and circles for their OT goals. If that is the case, you can have them draw the stems of flowers (simple lines) and glue on cut outs of flowers or shapes to create flowers. Make it simple, you know your little one best. Make accommodations as you both learn and always make it fun.

Kitchen

If you want to create a space in the kitchen for your child, feel free to follow these tips along with any unique adjustments your child may benefit from.

- Choose a low cabinet that can be for your little one's plates and cups.

- Be thoughtful in designating a spot your child can access independently.

- Be practical in choosing the items and activities that suit your child's interest and that they can engage in independently.

If your voyager is not an eager helper, but likes to be around you when you're in the kitchen, it is quite easy to create child-friendly spots around you. We have a bottom cabinet the kids can access, filled with activities like puzzles, board games, paper, and crayons. You may want to find a different spot and put actual kitchen gadgets you allow your child to play with, or provide items that keep your child busy while you're working in the kitchen. Having a small space for them is also great for working on independent skills, like accessing and putting away their own dishes; so, it may also be a good idea to have child dishes they can

handle. Needless to say, when we are in the kitchen, we are sure the items and activities in their special cabinet are things that interest them and they can do without our help, so as to not have so many interruptions while we focus on cooking and cleaning.

We have even gotten creative and placed red painter's tape on the kitchen floor to section off a few feet away from the stove. We have taught the girls that red tape is the boundary to keep them away from danger and they like to pretend its lava to keep them from getting too close to the stove! It becomes fun, especially for Victoria, and it encourages her imagination. It is amazing how tape can come in handy to make rules and boundaries clear.

Family Room

If you need to create a space in the family room for your child, feel free to follow these tips along with any unique adjustments your child may benefit from.

- Think about the uniqueness of your family and what makes them comfortable.

- Be open-minded to allow equipment if your child needs it (bean bag chairs, body sock, weighted blankets, etc.).

    - Consider having a basket with an activity that can bring the family together (books, games, etc.).

The place where families gather every evening is typically cozy and practical. In our family room, we placed two huge bean bags rather than coffee tables, so that the girls could jump and lay on. It keeps them from jumping on the furniture and also gives them a place where they can just be kids while the family is watching a movie, reading books out loud, or just having some great conversations. Also, Victoria will many times come up to us and ask for a hug or to crawl under one of the bean bags and in this way get what she is seeking, pressure! This calms her down and helps her focus in order to return to playtime or lessons. I know families that have a small trampoline or flybar in their space and others that keep toys in their playroom.

A great idea for this space is to also have a basket of books. In my opinion you can never have enough books in your home. When I feel the girls need a break from each other or just to change up the routine, we do quiet time in the living room; they each pick a spot and look through the books. It's such a great opportunity for you to sit with them to read. This fun and inviting place should be made right to fit in with you and your child's preferences.

As a parent, you know your family best. Look at the commonly used spaces in your home and make a list of things you could add or remove to accommodate the area, making it more practical and inviting for you and your child.

Spaces most used at home ?

Think about where you child spends the most time and what you would like those spaces to be for them.

Can you adjust the space and make it functional ?

Can I eliminate or add objects (furniture, toys, etc.) to make the space easy to navigate (ex. Objects can be found in three different baskets, making it easy for my child to find, use, and put away?

How will you use the spaces?

Will this be a space for teachable moments or is my main intention to keep my child safe and engaged while I attend to other tasks.

Possible adjustments ?

_____
_____
_____
_____
_____

 Every day is an opportunity

 Take a few breaths. Remind yourself: Are you calm and ready to work with your child?

 Seize that opportunity whenever possible and have fun.

CAPTAIN'S CHECKLIST

check off each space as you accommodate each room.

 Living Room/ Family Room

Playroom

 Kitchen

Navigating Autism From The Heart

- Meet them at their level: make sure to reflect and adjust your expectations to fit the needs of your voyager. Be patient, wait for them to show interest and follow their lead. Consider how they best make connections; by using visuals or songs, whether they need to touch and feel, etc.
- Brainstorm some of the ways to make this experience meaningful for your voyager: I take in account that Victoria is a visual learner. Preparing a story behind the reason we do a specific activity may help. you may use videos, books or visuals of why it is important. We talk about the activities like why its important and the steps on how to complete the activity.I use other visual aids like timers and verbal cues to help guide her step by step. If you do not want to provide verbal cues. Using a task strip depicting step by step of any activity is also beneficial. I motivate her and use things that interest her by presenting it as a game.
- Have a plan to make this connection and follow through: Once you brainstorm how you are going to teach the skill, setting a routine or creating a schedule will help you be consistent.

Now that we have created simple spaces for our voyagers, take a journey with me and give me the opportunity to show you how I help my voyagers navigate these spaces in practical ways to make simple connections.

Do you know about all my senses?

I actually have 7!

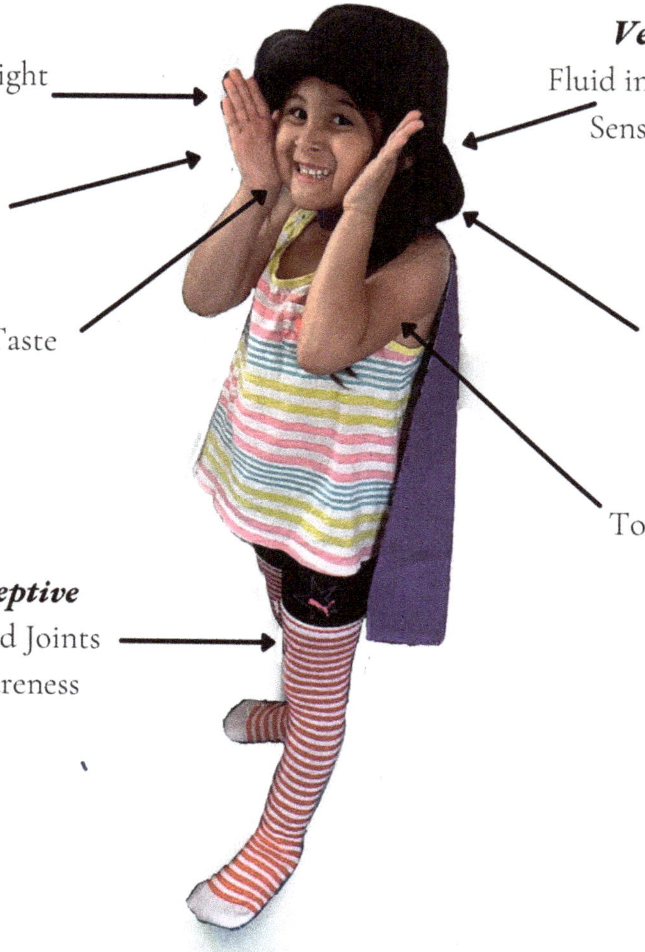

Sight

Smell

Taste

Vestibular
Fluid in the Ear Canal
Sense of Balance

Sound

Touch

Proprioceptive
-Muscels and Joints
Body Awareness

Sensory Diets are really important for me

-This helps me self regulate

-Get my sillies out

-Focus when I need to pay attention

-Help process the world around me

VOYAGERS AND SENSORY TIME

If there is one thing Victoria has taught us, it's feeling happiness. During our day-to-day busyness, sometimes we need a subtle reminder to stop and enjoy the little moments. Sensory time for our kids is just that; taking some time during our day to let off some steam, relax, or stretch out the stress we build up from school and work. Victoria's sensory diet is one of her favorite parts of the day. When she gets the sensorial input she needs, either

by playing or through quiet time, she can then self-regulate to keep working on her activities and to be present for much desired connections.

As seen in the sensory chart above, it's not just about the five senses we typically think of, but it's important to consider two more internal senses that play a key role in our children's development. There is so much more to our sensory processing that meets the eye. In *Understanding your child's Sensory Signals*, written by OT Angie Voss, OTR, Ms. Voss describes these two internal senses as being the proprioceptive and vestibular systems. The Vestibular system includes movement and balance, such as swinging, dancing or rolling over on a bounce ball. The Proprioceptive system incorporates body awareness; any push or pull movements and using our muscles and joints. Such senses are in use when performing heavy work, such as pushing a box of toys or pulling a full laundry basket. These physical activities are key in our child's development because strategically targeting it can help with focus, learning, and self- regulating skills.

Finally, Ms. Voss also describes the importance of our children's tactile senses, which is anything to do with touching the skin and the mouth, as well as touching textures like playdough, slime, or sand. Some children will seek pressure. It can present as the urge to squeeze or needing hard squeezes around their body to release tension. One of Victoria's challenges has been to learn how to seek pressure. She likes squeezing people's arms or pressing her chin into their neck or shoulders. This sensory seeking behavior can be inappropriate and intrusive, so she has learned to first make sure to approach a family member, such as ourselves or her grandparents. Secondly, she must ask permission to squeeze or press her chin on their shoulder. We continually teach her the importance of personal space with a "space invader game" ("don't be a space invader, keep one arm's distance from your neighbor!"), so that she knows not to approach another child on the playground or neighbor with this intention. We have been adamant about reminding her we only ask permission and seek pressure from family members, while emphasizing that we are never to ask this of friends, acquaintances, therapists, or strangers. When addressing these idiosyncrasies our children may have, it's crucial to have family support and to teach our children safety.

You can plan sensory opportunities or be spontaneous; your little one will let you know, via their behavior, when sensory time is needed. As a parent, I loved learning how our sensory system has such a great impact on how we learn and grow. Our children are lifelong learners, we must nurture this innate desire in them through fun sensory activities that help them keep focused and calm.

Sensory Time

Sensory Activity	When to do it?	Purpose
Swimming		
Going for a walk/run		
Jumping		
Playground Time		
Using a sensory bin: water/sand/rice		
Play-dough/ Therapuddy		
Quiet Time		
Dry-Brushing		
Compression/ Massage		

Create your sensory list here

 Every day is an opportunity

 Take a few breaths. Remind yourself: Are you calm and ready to work with your child?

 Seize that opportunity whenever possible and have fun.

Simple Connections

Sensory time does not need to be complicated. It can be super easy including swimming in a pool or soaking in a tub, going for a walk, jumping, rolling, and much more. It can also be creatively organized by you and your child's occupational therapist. Some voyagers may need more sensory input than others. Here are some ideas:

- Quiet space: This can be a tent, or pillows in a corner of a room; while maybe adding some essential oils and soft music help create a calming space. More discussion about quiet spaces will be in the following chapters

- Water play: Water is an easy and fun sensory medium to use with kids; it's one of Victoria's favorites. This can be as simple as bath time with bubbles and using a small container with different sized scoops and objects to play. A small child's pool or container filled with water beads or other interesting textures in water is relaxing for many and good old-fashioned swimming is also a great way to engage in sensory opportunities.

- Painter's tape: Create an obstacle course with painters tape. Add in animal walks like the crab and bear crawl, or "hop" like a bunny. Another fun idea is to use the tape to create streets for their toy cars to drive through. Any of these activities will provide good sensorial input for muscles and joints.

- Compression and massage: Sometimes squeezes just help settle their bodies. We are teaching Victoria to ask for pressure and hugs versus climbing on top of a family member to squeeze them without their permission. Massages may also be beneficial; we use unscented lotion and rub her back, arms, fingers, legs, and toes, which immediately has a calming effect.

- Dry Brushing: If your voyager is sensitive or aversive to touch, dry brushing may be very helpful. Please ask your OT about the Wilbarger Protocol. They can help determine if your child would benefit from this activity, which is simply brushing the skin lightly on certain points with a special body brush.

- Sensory Bins: These can hold amazing tactile activities, such as playing with sand, shaving cream, and anything else you can think of! You can put a lid on these for easy storage and later use. Sensory bins can be given themes by using different little toys or objects and changed out easily for specific learning opportunities. Refer to the Sensory Equipment section on page 86, for more examples.

VOYAGERS AND HOME ACTIVITIES

When we are home with our voyagers, every-day tasks, like getting the laundry done and cleaning up play areas, can be overwhelming at times. For some children, self- care routines, such as brushing their teeth and getting dressed, can also be a challenge. By creating a daily routine, your child can more easily learn and become accustomed to the task. In our case, we have found that embedding clean-up activities throughout the day has helped our daughters to clean up consistently and now it's a daily habit they enjoy doing.

If keeping a scheduled routine is challenging, then making the task a game or something fun to do when it comes up can take away that feeling of obligation. For example, when I ask Victoria to help me recycle trash, I make three piles, plastics/glass, cardboard and trash. I ask her to help me sort the trash. simply playing a word game like where does this milk cartoon belong? In the blue bin, yellow bin or trash? Until all the trash has been sorted out. When creating a simple schedule or a list of tasks that need to be done daily, you can also encourage your child to select the tasks and/ or the order in which they want to complete these tasks, allowing them some autonomy over their responsibilities.

Here are some suggestions to add to your daily routines or to make your tasks games.

Get ready to navigate!

Home Activities

Check your attitude	Is my child enjoying it?	Do I need to adapt the task?
Are you calm and in a positive frame of mind ?	Yes or No	Yes or No

Activities	Write in possible adaptations.
Placing dirty laundry away	
Sorting clothes for laundry day	
Tidying up	
Watering plants	
Washing dishes/ load dishwasher	
Putting dishes away/ unload dishwasher	
Recycling Trash	
Sweeping	
Vacuuming	

Create your own list here

Every day is an opportunity

Take a few breaths. Remind yourself: Are you calm and ready to work with your child?

Seize that opportunity whenever possible and have fun.

Simple Connections

- Placing dirty laundry: Keep a basket either in the bedroom or bathroom, preferably in the space your child dressed to minimize distractions. Have them place their dirty clothes in the basket after they change. Having a designated spot is great when tidying up around the house and finding clothes in the wrong places. Just remind your child, "Oh that doesn't belong there", "I wonder where it should go?" or "Oh the Laundry basket!".

- Sorting Clothes: You may want to start separating the clothes in three different piles. We sort light, dark, and color garments. I begin to sort and then give the girls turns, as I hand them pieces. I like to explain the process, as we are working, especially so that Victoria understands.

- Tidying Up: Simply take a few minutes throughout the day to put some things away from each space of your home. This helps you and your voyager stay organized. We have established a basic rule that enables us to more easily keep things in order; it is to simply clean up after each activity, before moving on to something else.

- Watering plants: This is a fun and easy activity for all kids. We have two different plants; one gets ice cubes once a week and the other gets watered the regular way. The girls enjoy taking turns throughout the week with these simple tasks. A watering can is not necessary, use what you have already at home, such as a cup!

VOYAGERS IN THE KITCHEN

The Kitchen is the most transited area in our entire home. It's where we spend time making memories by cooking meals, having little talks, and baking delicious treats our family enjoys. It gives us perfect opportunities to practice language, do more sensory activities, and learn important skills.

Here are some suggestions to add to your daily routines or to make your tasks games.

Kitchen

Check your attitude	Is my child enjoying it?	Do I need to adapt the task?
Are you calm and in a positive frame of mind ?	Yes or No	Yes or No

Activities	Write in possible adaptations.
Drying Dishes and silverware	
Putting away dishes and silverware	
Wiping down tables and chairs	
Prepping Snacks	
Putting away groceries	
Help with baking or cooking meals	
Play I spy: Work on identifying kitchen items.	
Fun with Food	

Create your own list here

Every day is an opportunity

Take a few breathes. Remind yourself: Are you calm and ready to work with your child?

Seize that opportunity whenever possible and have fun.

Simple Connections

- Drying dishes and silverware: Our two-year-old doesn't dry, but she does love to put things away. So, Victoria dry's their kid dishes and utensils, then passes it to her sisters to start sorting away and placing it in the kid's cabinet. Make

  a space in the kitchen so your child can have easy access. It's the small changes that have an impact; just make one simple change to include them in this process and watch your child blossom right in front of you.

- Wiping down tables and chairs: Of course, please use non-toxic solutions any time your kids are involved with cleaning. We use a small spray bottle with vinegar, water, and essential oils. If you have multiple kids, divide the responsibilities between them; one sprays the table and the other wipes down the surface. I also use cloth towels for two reasons; one is to be environmentally friendly and the second reason is kids hold the towel better than paper. It's a great fine and gross motor activity for busy hands.

- Putting away groceries: Be patient with this and only hand your child items they are able to handle. It's also a good opportunity to teach them to be gentle; for example, let them hold one egg and if it cracks, make it a great messy experiment! Have them help you clean it up and soon they will learn to be gentle with the egg and other delicate items. Otherwise, having your child store the items they like is a simple fun opportunity; for us, it's storing cookies, stacking cans, or placing yogurt cups in a drawer. Taking the fruit out and placing it in the fruit bowl is another easy and fun task. Be creative!

- Prep Snacks: Have your little voyager help you organize the snack drawer or the snack for the day. Victoria will ask for oranges and she will get her own bowl and napkin ready to eat her oranges. We are working on her independent skills, like peeling her own orange. So, I give her a partially peeled orange, so that she can work on this skill. Keep it simple for your child.   Have your child practice serving themself a yummy snack by scooping it from a container or bowl onto their own plate. You can even label the container with a number, so that your child can practice identifying numbers and also count the scoops.

- Help with baking or cooking meals: Now, I will admit, we rarely do this; but when we do, it is most likely to make breakfast or dessert. My voyager loves when she can help with making Arepas (Colombian corn patties) or make pancakes; baking is such a fun activity for her. She doesn't realize it, but she is learning important skills, such as following directions, math skills, strengthening independent living skills, and so much more. I usually set out the ingredients and utensils we need, then review the steps with Victoria in a simple manner; first, next, and last. We practice counting, rolling, and patting down to make shapes; great for sensory and hand manipulation. Her favorite part is definitely eating her creation, after she has worked so hard!

- Play I spy: This is great for labeling and identifying both familiar and unfamiliar items. It becomes a fun game to incorporate language. You can use the items in your kitchen or print pictures of the items, and even draw items if your voyager is an artist.

- Fun with Food: Pinterest and Google have some delicious and creative ideas that are easy to recreate, in order to expose picky eaters to different foods in a relaxed and playful manner. Start looking and find something new you want to try with your child. Remember it's about exposure and having fun; so, if your child doesn't want to try certain foods, it's fine as long as they participate in some way and enjoy the experience.

VOYAGERS IN THE BEDROOM

Morning routines are a simple way to add structure and opportunities for independence. The bedroom should be a clear clutter free area to relax. Creating such a space and encouraging independence starts with removing unnecessary items that could cause clutter and frustration. Keep it simple, have a spot for books, a few toys, their bed, a basket for dirty clothes, and maybe a shelf. Enabling our voyagers to keep their personal space tidy can help build on those self-care skills they will need throughout their lives.

Create your own list here

Bedroom Activities

Check your attitude	Is my child enjoying it?	Do I need to adapt the task?
Are you calm and in a positive frame of mind ?	Yes or No	Yes or No

Morning Routine	Write in possible adaptations.
Make Bed	
Change out of clothes	
Tidy up bedroom	
Go Potty	

Simple Connections

- Making the bed: This can be tricky depending on the age and size of your voyager. My girls are all under six years old, so I modify the process by helping them do some of it. I ask them to pull the comforter on their bed from corner to corner and straighten out their pillow. As they get older, I will add more steps to the process, like pulling bed sheets and folding the top of the bed cover. If your voyager can do more, provide modifications only if needed, which may be as minimal as keeping an eye on them as they complete it or to give them some reminders. Make it simple at first, then build on it.

- Change out of clothes: I have taught the girls when changing out of their pj's to place these under their pillow, so it can be used once more. When it is time to select an outfit, I remind the girls of the weather, so they consider appropriate dress. Victoria is now very good at picking out her own clothes. However, before she learned to dress herself independently, I would preselect two outfits to give her control over her choices and be able to select without feeling overwhelmed. Gradually, as she became accustomed to choosing, we increased her choices, until she was ready to choose from her closet. If your child needs help dressing, simply lay out the clothes on their bed and walk them step by step: pulling the shirt over their head, finding the holes to push one arm through and the next arm through. Some children may instinctively pull their clothes up, but if your child needs assistance, place your hand over theirs, so as to teach them what to do. As they get the hang of it then gradually remove yourself from the process. Have them sitting on the floor or bed to maintain balance, then proceed by having them slide one leg into one side of the pants and then the next leg. It is also a good idea to point out and teach where tags are located and how they help us in figuring out the right way to put our clothes on.

- Tidy up in the bedroom: Our girls play frequently in their bedroom! Because we have had silly accidents in the past (like tripping over shoes) and toys have gone missing; it gives me the opportunity to remind them the importance of tidying up daily. The areas they routinely organize are their personal items, dirty laundry, and clean laundry. The key is to have a clear designated place for each item they put away; in our case it is a laundry hamper, a toy basket, a small bookshelf, and drawers for clothes. This eliminates confusion and enables the girls to successfully clean up when the room is messy.

VOYAGERS ON FAMILY OUTINGS

It is crucial to involve our voyager in community activities as much as possible. New places can be very scary, anxiety-inducing, uncomfortable, or plain boring situations for our child. When we are out running errands, visiting a library, exploring a museum, or visiting with family and friends, these can be difficult or overwhelming for Victoria. It is many times rooted in her lack of interest and discomfort in participating in activities or being around too many people; she

may whine or cry, maybe even have an anxiety attack, ask to leave, or need one of her sensory gadgets, like headphones or hand fidgets to get through the moment. It may sound excessive and keeping her home would be the easier route. However, this is what hinders her, and most children on the spectrum, from successfully integrating in the community. We can reduce our child's anxiety and more easily encourage positive experiences, while visiting unfamiliar places with certain accommodations in place.

As you plan outings, make sure to bring a "survival backpack" for your voyager. This will be unique to each child and can contain comfort items, such as a favorite toy, headphones to minimize noise, a calming blanket, snacks, drinks, and any other item that is sure to help calm them. Think out of the box if you need to, as you know your little one best. Planning ahead is key to making the child's experience pleasant, as well as giving yourself peace of mind.

However, there is no guarantee! Once, on a routine grocery trip, what seemed to be a regular non-eventful day turned upside down. Our grocery store ran out of the specific pizza crust we usually purchased for Victoria. When we walked down the frozen aisle and didn't see the pizza crust in its usual place, my daughter lost it. She started screaming and crying at the top of her lungs. I was by myself with my three girls, all under the age of six, and all I could do was try to calm her down with my soft suggestions, but it was to no avail. So, I picked her up and walked straight to the cashier lane to pay for the few things in our cart. Once we got in the car, she was able to calm down, as I guided her through breathing and counting, and reviewed pictures of feelings we had used on previous occasions. This took a few minutes and although it was inconvenient that we didn't finish shopping, it truly was the best outcome for Victoria to learn and practice self-regulating her emotions. We have had vacations, birthday parties, holidays, special field trips, and other events cut short or canceled, in order to prioritize addressing our daughter's needs. If this is something you have experienced, know you are not alone. As frustrating as this may be, we continue to move forward, always preparing as best we can. Sometimes, I do wish I could go shopping like any normal person, but that's simply not my life. I have learned to take each moment and appreciate it as it comes, and she has gradually learned to manage her anxiety and be more patient, as well as much more flexible when visiting new places or when there is a change in routine.

Here are some tools and suggestions to make outing happy, safe, and as stress-free as possible for our young explorers.

Family Outings

Check your attitude	Is my child enjoying it?	Do I need to adapt the activity?
Are you calm and in a positive frame of mind ?	Yes or No	Yes or No

Outing	Write in possible adaptations.
Grocery Store	
Library	
Church/Place of worship	
School	
Playground	
Movie Theater	
Theme Park	
Concert	
Family / Friends Home	

Create your own list here

 Every day is an opportunity

 Take a few breathes. Remind yourself: Are you calm and ready to work with your child?

 Seize that opportunity whenever possible and have fun.

Simple Connections

- Library: When visiting the library, set the expectation on how many books you will check out and how long you will be in the library. Also, set two or three simple rules that enable your child to behave appropriately while there; for example, use gentle hands, stay close to mommy, and use inside voices. When we go to our weekly library visits, I have to remind Victoria to choose different books, as she tends to become a bit obsessive over My Little Pony comic books; her getting upset is inevitable when she doesn't find the particular book she wants. Now we use themes, based on holidays or what we are learning in our homeschool, as a guide when searching for books. My Little Pony stories are off limits for now, until Victoria is emotionally ready. The first day we avoided her favorite comic books was difficult, to say the least. We left the library upset and without books. We were consistent and continued to redirect her to theme books on each visit and now it is much easier for her to accept the weekly change in books.

- Visiting with family and friends: A variety of things to help this outing be successful; bring their favorite snacks or meals, sensory gadgets and comfort items. Remind your child why you are visiting and to let you know when they are ready to go. If your voyager can tell time, let them know the time you will be heading home. If your voyager needs a timer, set your phone's alarm or their watch. If they get anxious, find a spot where you can practice calming down. Two things can happen; your voyager calms down and tries to enjoy the visit or it will be time to go. In our family, we made the decision long ago to accept these outcomes. It doesn't happen often, but we need to honor and validate Victoria's specific needs.

- Playground: I have set two requirements prior to visiting any playground; the playground needs to be gated and have restrooms nearby. I cannot yet trust that Victoria would not walk away; if she sees a dog or bird, she will run outside the playground towards it. So, safety First!

SURVIVAL BACKPACK CHECKLIST

- ☐ Head Phones
- ☐ Blanket
- ☐ Favorite Toy
- ☐ Sun Glasses
- ☐ Social Story

- ☐ Snacks
- ☐ Drink
- ☐ Timer
- ☐ Fidgets

Here are some suggestions for family outings and trips into the community!

- Talk about unfamiliar outings by using a social story, showing pictures of the things you will see and do, or looking up the place on the internet to virtually explore prior to your visit. Don't overwhelm your child with too much information, just the highlights.

- Use a timer or clock to let them know how long the visit will be.

- Remember to give your little one time to process the environment and remember not all outings will turn out smoothly. It is essential to praise our child for the effort they are making, no matter the outcome. The most important thing to bear in mind is that our children, deep inside, want to connect and be part of the world. Though they may not show it, we serve as the ones that help them bridge the gap early on.

- If your outing is cut short, do not allow yourself to be disappointed. I know first hand how upsetting it can be to end a visit early, especially if it involves a family reunion. Here is where being strategic can help; for example, making sure you have special items in the "survival backpack" or having ready anything else you are sure your child will enjoy and can do while on the visit.

- Practice safety whenever you go out into the community. I am constantly teaching safety; look both ways before crossing the street, hold hands in busy places, and stay close to mommy! I normally have a long purse strap hanging off my shoulder for my girls to hold, because Victoria doesn't like to hold hands. She might hold the strap or a belt loop on my pants, while I hold hands with her sisters. If I am going to a busy place, I will put my two-year-old in the stroller and have Victoria and Veronica hold a side of the stroller.

VOYAGERS AT BATHROOM TIME

Hygiene is a very important skill for our voyagers to learn. Bathing, brushing her teeth, and combing her hair have been challenges in our home with Victoria. These tasks were very uncomfortable and even scary at times for her. Like in previous examples, turning these tasks into fun games eased Victoria's anxiety and allowed for her to complete her bathroom routine with minimal directions.

Here are some suggestions to add to your daily routines or to make your tasks games

Bathroom Time

Check your attitude	Is my child enjoying it?		Do I need to adapt the activity?		
Are you calm and in a positive frame of mind ?	Yes	or	No	Yes	or	No

Evening Routine	Write in possible adaptations.
Showering /Bathing	
BrushingTeeth	
Using Toilet	
Combing hair	
Washing hands	

Create your own list here

 Every day is an opportunity

 Take a few breathes. Remind yourself: Are you calm and ready to work with your child?

 Seize that opportunity whenever possible and have fun.

Simple Connections

- Bathing: Have things in your bathroom that build independence; a towel (preferably a favorite color or character for drying off), a washcloth to help rub soap on, toys that won't distract but help keep your voyager calm and happy, light scented soaps and shampoos if your child is sensitive to smells, etc. Also consider a removal shower head or rinsing cup, which they can learn to maneuver themselves. When it's time to shower or bathe, if your child is like mine, the challenge was not getting in the tub; it was washing her hair. She was terrified of water going in her nose. In the beginning, I forced this step on her and the results were not pleasant. Her trust dissipated. I quickly realized that I needed to take my time rather than get through motions. I turned bath time into a game by role- playing with her doll; showing her how to soap it up and then soaping her up immediately after. We used her doll as an example for every step of the bathing routine, including shampooing and rinsing. It was a long process, but it helped Victoria understand the goal. Since my daughter responds to silliness, I always started our baths with "pee-yew, you're stinky!" and ended bath time with "mmmm, now you smell fresh and clean!". When your voyager is having a difficult time bathing, take a step back and let them know they are safe by first connecting with them.

- Brushing Teeth: This is not an easy task; so, when Victoria brushes her teeth, we use an hourglass timer and a light-up toothbrush to entice her to a race. I take out the timer and light-up toothbrush with toothpaste already on it and say, "on your mark, get set, go!". Then we flip the hourglass and enthusiastically call out different brushing positions; "brush the top teeth, now the bottom, next the sides, and don't forget that stinky tongue!". She thinks it's hilarious, as she attempts to brush her teeth on her own; but then she is relaxed enough so I can then ask her permission to help; I follow through and gently finish up brushing her teeth. Another possibility is to have a visual strip for each step and guide them through the routine by pointing to each picture, as the steps are to be completed.

- Using the Toilet: No matter what stage of toileting your child may be in, have these things available in your bathroom to help build independence. Include a step stool to reach the toilet seat, a child seat for little voyagers, and toilet paper easily accessible. In our case, we began toilet training Victoria when she was almost three years old by using the time training method. Because she was non-verbal at the time, we had visuals, vegan chocolate chips to motivate and praise her when she was successful, lots of changing clothes, and a timer. In the beginning, she may not have been completely aware of what we were doing, but she eventually got into the routine; going first thing in the morning and 20 minutes after eating a meal or drinking. Additionally, we took her to the bathroom each time prior to leaving the house and then again when we arrived at our destination (grocery store, therapy, etc.). It took her roughly four weeks to realize she had control of her bladder; every accident served as a great learning experience. She did not like being wet and definitely didn't like changing out of her favorite outfit. As she became more aware of her body and the toileting process, she grew confident. It seemed like a long three months before it really clicked for her and she walked to the bathroom and went without telling anyone. She let us know that day by yelling loudly and signing "all done" with her hands!

VOYAGERS AND SLEEP TIME ROUTINE

A good sleep time routine is as important as incorporating daily sensory activities. As we have previously discussed, having a simple sensory routine can ease your child's day; however, this goes hand in hand with proper sleep. If our voyagers are not getting their full hours of sleep, they are more likely to succumb to emotional and behavioral difficulties the next day. In our household, our girls know that once mommy and daddy say the magic words, "it's time to get ready for bed"; we mean business! Getting them to  sleep at a decent hour after completing a routine; for example, drinking a cup of milk, changing into pj's, brushing teeth, and using the toilet, can sometimes be challenging. However, for us it's crucial we do it EVERY NIGHT, why? because we have learned that keeping a consistent bedtime routine has a significant impact on our girls' success.

Whether it is intentional or not! The thing about a bedtime routine is that everyone has one. If you have a wonderful thing going, don't change what's working already; but, if you feel there is room for improvement, the list below can help you create or improve your routine.

Bed Time

Check your attitude	Is my child enjoying it?	Do I need to adapt the activity?
Are you calm and in a positive frame of mind ?	Yes or No	Yes or No

Evening Routine	Write in possible adaptations.
Announce "Its time to get ready for bed"	
Serve their last cup of milk/water	
Time to tidy up	
Brush Teeth	
Go Potty	
Change Into PJ's	
Story time	
Prayers/Goodnight songs/Hugs	

Create your own list here

 Every day is an opportunity

 Take a few breathes. Remind yourself: Are you calm and ready to work with your child?

 Seize that opportunity whenever possible and have fun.

Simple Connections

- CONSISTENCY is an essential part of adopting a routine. For example, we begin our routine around 7:15 PM every night by making the "bedtime" announcement. We first put our two-year-old to bed; to my bed, that is! (Side note: we've co-slept with each of our girls in their early years, giving them the comfort and freedom to transition to their own rooms when they feel ready!) By 7:30, when our little one is sound asleep, my older girls have had time to wind down and are ready to begin the simple evening tasks listed above. This may not be what is recommended by experts, but it is what works for our family on a daily basis and seems easiest for our girls to follow and enjoy.

- BE CLEAR when you announce bedtime and remember to check your own state of mind. Take deep breaths if you think this will be challenging, mentally prepare to take it slow, and remember how important this will be toward your child's progress. Announce bedtime by singing a familiar tune each night, by simply saying it, or find any other way to enable your child to recognize this each evening. Give your child a few moments to process in their mind that the day is ending. If your kids happen to be anything like mine on occasion, remind yourself the crying and complaining is temporary. Take a moment to reassure them their toys, movies, and activities will be there waiting the next day and all activities can be continued. Consistently saying this to Victoria has eased anxieties over not having finished an activity or playing during the day. The key here is to calmly acknowledge frustrations and help the child solve the problem or find an alternative.

- ADDRESS NEEDS immediately after announcing the routine. I consider this to be the last chance for my girls to snack or drink. They enjoy almond-milk; giving our voyagers something soothing and pleasant helps relax them. Having them drink at this point gives them enough time, in our case, to be ready to empty their bladders by the end of our Storytime. (Let's reduce the chances of having nighttime accidents!)

- TIDYING UP is an important habit. Since my kids are always in their playroom, this space can be a perpetual mess. Again, we sing a clean-up song and I start helping them clean up; as long as they are participating by putting some things away, I consider it a win! Take into perspective that as they get older, they will do more if you are consistent with the routine. Keep the main goal in mind and remember their tidying will not be perfect.

- POTTY TIME, as we call it, is different for each family depending on your child. Victoria, for example, wore a diaper to bed until she was about 4 years old, as a preventative measure, despite being trained. We had used time-training in her early years, until she got into the habit of going right before bed. This strategy of taking her to the bathroom on timed intervals throughout the day, helped her to become aware and to eventually go to the bathroom on her own. Immediately after, while working on hand washing, I take the opportunity to remind Victoria we will brush her teeth next.

- HYGIENE is one of our greatest struggles! For six years, and counting, brushing Victoria's teeth continues to be a work in progress. My voyager has sensory issues inside her mouth that make her sensitive to the flavor and scent of some toothpastes and the brushing sensations. Fortunately, we have found a natural, mild-tasting, fluoride-free toothpaste that is safe for her to swallow; as she's not yet able to rinse her mouth properly. We also give her the option to choose her toothbrush each evening, including an electric toothbrush, a traditional toothbrush, and even a three-sided brush; she chooses depending on her sensitivity that particular day. Between ages 2 and 4 Victoria used a visual task strip, and watched YouTube videos like Elmo's teeth brushing song to help her learn the sequence. Currently, she just needs reminders to fully brush and we may even play a game to make it fun. As previously discussed, I do ask her permission to help her finish brushing her teeth, to make sure her mouth is clean. Asking her helps to build trust and credibility. Many times, she has denied my help and I have in these instances given her extra water to rinse rather than insisting.

- CHANGING into pajamas can be fun for many voyagers. If they are having a difficult time, allowing your child to choose their own sleepwear, not limited to actual pajamas, may help motivate. This has certainly helped my girls transition happily into bedtime. Before changing for the night, make sure to keep a laundry hamper nearby and encourage your child to put their clothes in; remember you are encouraging organization throughout every part of the home with these simple steps.

- STORYTIME helps to relax our voyagers and end the day on a positive note. We sometimes read our weekly library books, because the girls get really excited about these. They can also choose from favorite classic chapter stories that are familiar to them; for example, Alice in Wonderland and Peter Pan. We have read the same stories for weeks sometimes! I have found this to give my girls something fun to look forward to each night. Wordless picture books are also a favorite choice, as these allow for personalization in narrating a longer or a shorter story.

- AMBIENCE after reading is a must for us; we sometimes turn on soothing sounds, such as ocean waves or rainfall. A night light is also essential; our oil diffuser serves as a night light and it has the option to add calming scents that also help the girls relax into sleep. Use your discretion in regards to the level of ambiance your voyager may require and avoid it if it becomes a distraction!

- FLEXIBILITY can be challenging. In all honesty, some nights we are strict with the routine and other nights we alter the schedule by adding or skipping the non-essential steps, depending on how the girls are doing. Sometimes Victoria will become overly attached to routines and this is when we intentionally change things up! We keep calm in preparing for such a night, knowing she will have some difficulty. In our case, we feel it important to have her break from rigidity at times, in order to teach her to be flexible. This may not be feasible for many voyagers; it will be up to you to do what is best for your family.

SETTING THE MOOD

One

Have them pick out there own PJ's

TWO

Timer's are your friend. Visuals are great help to transition from one activity to another.

THREE

Soft Music -Lullubies, instrumental music or nature songs can be very helpful in setting the mood for bed time.

FOUR

Night-lights are a great tool. Our night light doubles as a diffuser. Use lavender or frankincense essential oils for a calm and relaxing bedtime.

FIVE

Stick to your bedtime routine. Consistency is the key

Navigating Autism
From The Heart

Thank you for taking this journey with me and allowing me to share our family's journey with you. Navigating autism can be trialling; but with an open mind, a willingness to change perspectives, a positive attitude, and the love you have for your voyager, the possibiities are wonderfully endless!
I am so excited for the steps you are taking to learn and grow in becoming the best teacher and advocate for your amazing child!
I believe in you!
You Got This! Every day is an opportunity , make those beautiful SIMPLE CONNECTIONS with your child. They are waiting for you!

 -Angie

RECOMMENDATIONS AND REFERENCES

Simple Connections Equipment

Painters Tape

Obstacle course: In the pictures below, I created a path for Victoria to follow on her bike. This helps support body awareness and balance. Painters tape can be used to create hopscotch game, which can be very easy or challenging.

Visual Barrier : You can put visual reminders of areas to avoid, like a hot stove. In the kitchen, I taped the space separating where Victoria can stand and where she must avoid. In this case, the tape represents lava that Victoria must avoid. This is a great way to visually in force safety rules in a fun way.

Bicycle Course

Obstacle Course

Visual Barrier

Sensory Bin

Fill up bins: Fill up bins with different materials, such as water, cotten balls, shredded paper, sand, water beads or jello. So many fun ideas, get creative!

Use objects: I like to add different toys or objects into the bins, like small dinosaurs. In this picture, I have a wooden puzzle board with shapes. Victoria searches for the missing pieces in the purple kinetic sand and puts the puzzle together.

Play-Dough

For busy hands: Work on cutting, rolling out shapes, letters, numbers, and counting. This single activity can provide so many sensory benefits, such as tactile, proprioceptive, and visual input . When manipulating, the play-dough you can add essential oils to enhance the activity. Cutting , pulling, rolling, and squishing provides proprioceptive input.

Indoor Swing

Swinging: Swinging is a fantastic way to get vestibular input. This provides for some relaxing and calming effects. The swing is also great to be used for a quiet space, and reading a nook. This is a tool that needs supervision. Never leave your child unattended .

Fun

References

Libutti, A (2015) *Awakened by Autism: Embracing Autism, Self, and Hope for a New World.* Hay House Inc.

Kaufman, R.K. (2015) *Autism Breakthrough: The Groundbreaking Method that Has Helped Families All Over the World.* St. Martin's Griffin, Illustrated Edition

Voss, A (2011) *Understanding Your Child's Sensory Signals: A Practical Use Handbook for Parents and Teachers.* (3rd ED.) CreateSpace Independent Publishing

Inspirational and Informative Books

The following books have been amazing tools in my journey with my daughter. When you find time, I recommend considering this list. This collection is inspirational and full of wisdom and ideas for families like ours.

Autism and The God Connection: Redefining the Autistic Experience Through Extraordinary Accounts of Spiritual Giftedness by William Stillman

Autism Breakthrough: The Groundbreaking Method that Has Helped Families All Over the World by Raun K. Kaufman

Autistic Logistics: A Parents' Guide to Tackling Bedtime, Toilet Training, Tantrums, Meltdowns, Hitting, and Other Everyday Challenges by Kate Wilde

Awakened by Autism: Embracing Autism, Self, and Hope for a New World by Andrea Libutti

Look Me in the Eye: My Life with Asperger's by John Elder Robison

Sensational Kids: Hope and Help for Children with Sensory Processing Disorder by Lucy Jane Miller, PHD, OTR

Son-Rise: The Miracle Continues by Barry Neil Kaufman

The Out-of-Sync Child: Recognizing and Coping with Sensory Processing Disorders by Carol Kranowitz

The Reason I Jump: The Inner Voice of a Thirteen-Year-Old Boy with Autism by Naoki Higashida

Thinking in Pictures: My Life with Autism by Temple Grandin

Understanding Your Child's Sensory Signals: A Practical Use Handbook for Parents and Teachers by Angie Voss OTR